G000245471

Standing and watching the activity of a spring garden can give an idea of the incredible range of plants and animals that inhabit our planet. Many people feel a sense of wonder and awe when they look closely at the natural world, observing the beauty and colour around them. Even though we may get to know names and life styles of many living things, do we notice a sense of order in nature? At first glance, much of what we see appears haphazard. In fact, the shapes of living things are functional, helping the species to survive.

The natural world has developed patterns and forms which are marvels of efficiency and beauty, as in the aerodynamics of birds' wings or in the strong hexagonal compartments of honeycombs. Nature takes shape, *through photographs and illustrations, describes many examples of the mathematics that occurs in nature.*

Acknowledgments

The authors and publishers wish to acknowledge illustrative material as follows:

Illustrations

Pages 8, 15, 16, 17, 19, 22, 23, 29, 32, 33, 35, 37, 43, 44, 45, 49, 50 and 51 are by Graham Marlow; pages 26, 38-39 by Christine Owen. The pictures of bridges on pages 49 and 51 are from the Ladybird Book *Leader Bridges*.

Photographs

Cover, endpaper and pages 4, 7 (1 and 8), 9 (bottom), 11 (bottom), 13, 18-19, 24 (fossil), 25, 26, 33, 40-41, 42 by Tim Clark; page 22, Bruce Coleman Ltd; page 17, French Government Tourist Office; pages 6, 8, 10, 13 (watch), 20, 21 (top and bottom left), 27, 34, 47, 48 (right) by John Moyes; pages 5, 7 (2, 4 and 6), 9 (top), 11 (centre left), 12, 14, 21 (bottom right), 28, 31 (top left and top right), 32, 33, 46 from the Natural History Photographic Agency; page 16, Oxford Scientific Films Ltd; pages 11 (top) and 23 by John Paull; page 50, Sea Containers Services Ltd; page 7 (3 and 7) by Seaphot Ltd; pages 11 (centre right), 24 (flowers), 31 (centre and bottom) by Harry Stanton; pages 7 (5), 24 (starfish), 48 (left) by M M Whitehead.

Nature
takes shape

by John *and* Dorothy Paull

Ladybird Books Loughborough

LOOKING AT NATURE

If you stand in a city park or by a stream in the countryside early one spring morning and look around, you will see a fabulous array of colours, shapes, sizes and movement. There are numerous varieties of flowers with beautifully coloured petals, shrubs and bushes covered with fragrant blossom, towering trees with patterned bark and pointed leaves. Delicately coloured butterflies, wasps and bees flit gracefully and purposefully from flower to flower. In the dead leaves and soil a myriad of small creatures go about their work, such as ants fetching and carrying, spiders waiting in taut, sticky webs, millipedes, centipedes and beetles scurrying from the light. Beneath them, under the earth, more fascinating creatures of various forms are to be found. All have exquisite form. It seems as if their intricacy is designed to please the human eye.

This beauty and tranquillity, the delights of nature, inspires artists and poets to paint pictures

and write poems that stand the test of time. Yet there is much more to the natural world. There is mathematics – the Mathematics of Nature. Nature is a master builder.

When artists and poets admire a rose or a robin, they are really admiring a mathematically efficient living machine. If you look closely, it is noticeable that the rose's petals and the robin's feathers grow in definite patterns. Each and every part of the flower and bird has purpose and reason. It is not there just to look beautiful and please the human eye.

The shapes and patterns of living things are functional, helping species to survive. Long ago, brilliant Greek mathematicians like Pythagoras, Archimedes and Euclid looked at nature's ingenious use of geometry in the growth of plants and the shapes of animals, and developed a mathematical understanding of shape and form that inspired their art and building. This feature of the environment, the Mathematics of Nature, has since affected the work of scientists, architects and engineers in many different ways.

GEOMETRIC SHAPES AROUND US

All the plants, insects, birds and animals that inhabit the land, sky and sea, are the results of millions of years of evolution. Their shapes have changed gradually over the years, improving as they adapt and alter to fit in with the changing environment. After a lifetime of research, the great student of nature, Charles Darwin, pointed out that if living things do not alter when change is required, they become extinct. This process is happening even now. Man's small toe is of little use to him. Perhaps, in thousands of years' time, it will disappear altogether.

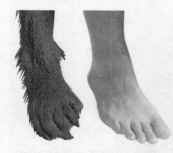

Monkey's foot   *Man's foot*

Even though the shapes of plants and animals can be very different — for instance, the striking contrast between a horse and a slug, or a humming bird and an octopus — all forms of life have shapes that conform to basic geometric laws.

Nature's designs are ingenious. The more unusual and weird shapes that we see in the wild are just extensions of simpler, more familiar ones: circles, triangles and squares, which are simple, efficient and strong shapes.

1 Crab   2 Orchid   3 Octopus   4 Dragonfly   5 Lizard
6 Cactus   7 Jellyfish   8 Daffodil   ▶

Circles

Plato, a famous observer of nature who lived in Greece about 400 BC, called the circle the perfect shape. It dominates our world. Looking around us, where do we see circles in Nature? We see through eyes that are round. All animals' eyes are this shape because it is simple, strong and ideal for the purpose of seeing.

We live on a magnificent circle, the Earth. The Earth, a three-dimensional circle or sphere, is one of the solar family of nine circular planets that revolve round the sun in elliptical orbits. An *ellipse* is an oval — a flattened circle. Six of the planets have circular satellites or moons that move around them in an ellipse.

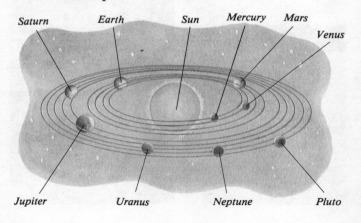

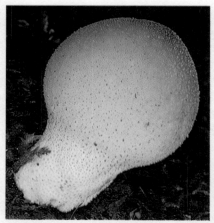

If we look closer at hand, what can we find that is circular in shape? The trunks of trees and the arrangement of petals on flowers are circular. Most woodland toadstools that grow in vast numbers in early autumn, when conditions are ideal, are circular in shape. One in particular, the Puffball (shown above), is *spherical* (like a small ball).

In the sea, the spiny sea urchin (below, left) is spherical, and in ponds and canals the minute rotifer is just one of many microscopic animals that are circular. Plant seeds are usually round, as are many of our fruit and vegetables.

Looking for circles Sometimes circles are made accidentally in the countryside. Marram grass, which grows successfully on sand dunes because it can resist violent winds, strong sunlight and salty sea spray, makes circles in the sand. The wind swirls the drooping leaf blades which cut a trail in the damp sand. Farm gates wear out a semi-circle in mud after being opened and dragged through the ground.

Hibernation Many wild animals make circles with their bodies when they curl up to sleep in holes or in the undergrowth. Domestic cats make an almost perfect circle when they rest in front of a roaring fire. This position has purpose and is not chosen just for comfort. It reduces the amount of the cat's body that is exposed to the air, and prevents the cat losing too much body heat.

Hibernating animals like squirrels conserve body heat by tucking up into a ball during their long winter sleep.

Fossil sea snail (Ammonite)

The timid hedgehog (*above*) curls up when attacked, and this acts as a good defence against predators. The pill louse (*shown left*), a relative of the woodlouse, wraps itself into a ball when threatened by voracious centipedes, and the shape makes it difficult to bite. Chitons (primitive sea snails), act in a similar way when attacked by fish.

One of the most unusual forms of the circle in nature is made by honey-bees. The honey they make is stored in small *hexagonal* (six-sided) compartments in the honeycomb. It is thought that the bee does not deliberately make the hexagon-shaped storage area, but rather makes circular stores which are squeezed together, forming the hexagons. Hexagons *tessellate* (that is, they fit together without having any spaces), so that thousands of units can be fitted into the honeycomb without wasting any space.

The Wheel The circle is indispensable to man, too. The circular shape we call the wheel is considered one of man's greatest discoveries. Life as we know it would come to an abrupt halt if our machines were suddenly deprived of its simple and efficient shape. Nearly every machine you can think of has a wheel somewhere in its design.

Triangles

The triangle shape is often found in the natural world. Many trees, especially conifers, are triangle-shaped. This allows the sunlight to reach the bottom branches and leaves or needles. Some tree leaves, like the birch (*right*), are triangular.

A Douglas Fir

Many kinds of fish, particularly the ray and the shark, are triangular in form. Fish scales, too, are triangular and their placement follows a definite pattern.

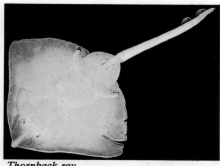
Thornback ray

Over the centuries, builders have used the triangle shape because of its strength and beauty. The classic examples are the Pyramids (*below*) built by the Egyptians in 3000 BC, amazingly without any mathematical aids. The masons who built our churches and cathedrals in the middle ages used the arch and the triangle frequently, and their robust and beautiful buildings are still used today, a testimony to the strength of the triangle.

Squares

No one has yet discovered a square animal or square plant! However, the shape does occur, especially in the proportions of larger animals.

There are chemicals that have square crystal shapes. Table salt and sugar are in crystal form and can easily be seen with a magnifying glass.

Sugar crystals

The stems of wild plants appear in all shapes and sizes. If we look at the forms of the cross sections of stems we can find examples of the three basic geometric shapes:

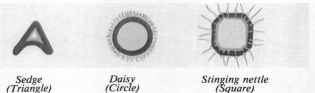

Sedge (Triangle)   *Daisy (Circle)*   *Stinging nettle (Square)*

The arch shape – Pont du Gard aqueduct (Roman)

Just as plants, insects and animals use geometry in their struggle for existence, man too builds shapes that follow the pattern of nature's geometry, protecting him from the weather and giving him comfort and security, as well as designs that please him. In early cultures, the Greeks used rectangular designs, the Egyptian Pyramids were based on triangles, and the Romans introduced the arch, which is part of a circle. On a less grand scale, the basic geometric designs are also obvious in the American Indian tepee, the Eskimo's igloo, and the Spanish American adobe.

Tepee (Triangle)   *Igloo (Circle)*   *Adobe (Square)*

17

EARLY MAN'S USE OF GEOMETRY

The geometric shapes that nature produced in
living things to ensure survival were recognised by
early man. Archaeologists excavating early man's cave
dwellings have discovered pottery and basketwork
decorated with designs based on circles, triangles
and squares. They have uncovered stone tools and
war weapons which are symmetrical and triangular
in shape. They were made this way because they
travelled through the air faster and straighter,
giving the hunter more chance of hitting his prey.

The first prehistoric man to use a natural object
like a flint as a weapon probably had no firm idea
in mind about its shape. After gathering a heap of
flint chips around him, he tried each one until he
found one best suited for the purpose he had in
mind. That shape was then copied by members of
his tribe, and the idea soon spread to other groups.

If you look at museum displays of stone age tools and weapons, you will see a striking likeness between those from different parts of the world. Arrowheads from England have the same shape as those found in America. The arrowhead shape is the most efficient for its function. Other weapons that developed from the original discovery of the arrow are called *logical shapes* because they are the result of man's thinking about them before they were made.

Extreme left –
Stone age arrowheads;
centre – badger's skull;
right – medieval helmet.

Some early helmets had a ridge on top. Did this design perhaps come about because someone noticed the hard ridge on the back of a badger's skull? As the badger is a burrowing animal, the ridge protects it from earth falls as it digs underground. If early man deliberately used this design, we have another example of a logical shape.

SYMMETRY

One of the most important mathematical characteristics in the natural world is *symmetry*. A shape is symmetrical when the mirror image of one side appears on the other side to form the complete shape. Put more simply, many creatures can be divided down the middle into two halves that match each other.

Symmetry gives a living thing perfect balance or harmony, because the body proportions are equal. If a butterfly's body was not symmetrical it

Butterfly

would not be able to fly. A lizard's legs would be useless if they were different sizes. Imagine ourselves with one arm two metres longer than the other!

Leaves of trees, bushes and flowers with central veins are symmetrical. Cut these leaves along the middle vein and you have two identical parts. The pattern of leaf growth on ash tree branches (*below*) is symmetrical.

Leaves are normally constant in shape. For example, even though there are several kinds of oaks and maples, the leaf shape is generally the same in each species. This means that all oaks and maples of different species normally look alike. Leaf shapes are useful and reliable clues to identifying the parent plant. *Botanists* (people who study plants) can be shown a single leaf and recognise the tree or plant from which it came.

Maple

Oak

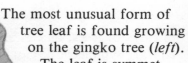

The most unusual form of
tree leaf is found growing
on the gingko tree (*left*).
The leaf is symmet-
rical and triangular
or fan-shaped and
is unlike any other
flowering plant or
tree. The gingko is
unique because it is
the only survivor
of a tree family that
flourished millions of years ago in the age of
dinosaurs, long before the development of the trees
we know today. It is not affected by air pollution
and grows well in our cities and parks.

The sassafras tree from the North American
continent has three different-shaped leaves (*below*)

that grow on the same branch. Ivy, too, is unusual. Ivy leaves are *polymorphic*, which means that there are many varieties of form. This helps the ivy as the leaves fit together like a mosaic when they cling to a brick wall or wooden fence (*see below, left*). Each leaf then gets the full amount of light possible from the sun.

Whatever shape the leaves take, however, the purpose of the leaf is to manufacture food for the tree. Leaves are called 'sugar factories' because they produce all the food the tree needs in the form of sugar. The leaves' jagged edges help to evaporate the water used in the food making process (called *photosynthesis*), they reduce the wind resistance, and they act as 'drip tips' for shedding excess water.

Ivy

Oak leaf

Stem allows leaf to flutter without snapping

Drip tips which act as rain spouts

Irregular leaf shape increases surface area

23

THE PENTAGON

One of the most famous mathematicians of all time was a Greek called Pythagoras, a man fascinated by the geometry he saw in nature. Pythagoras and his followers had a secret society. They studied geometry as if it were a religion. Their secret sign was a five-sided figure, a *pentagon*, a shape that occurs in nature. Five-sided forms are frequently found among plants but are quite rare in the animal kingdom except for some sea creatures such as the starfish. Every starfish begins life as a five-sided embryo. The pentagon shape gives them strength to resist the buffeting of the waves.

The five divisions of the sea urchin at the left

Echinoderm fossil (primitive sea urchin)

Violet

Starfish

SPIRALS

The spiral is a beautiful shape. Perhaps the best example of nature's spiral is the whorl on the shells of snails. Numerous varieties of snails crawl in the undergrowth in woods, fields and gardens, and forage in the bottom of ponds and canals. The homes of these interesting creatures are made from calcium and are all perfect spirals, so precise that they might have been constructed by mathematicians. Thousands of different sea snails have spiral shells. Sea shell shops have baskets full of exotic species, like the nautilus, the auger, whelks, and cone shells.

The spirals of these shells are right-handed. That is, looked down on from the top, the spiral revolves in a clock-wise direction. Very occasionally, the spiral is left-handed, called a *sinistral spiral*. This is very

Lightning Whelk showing sinistral spiral

rare. Some species, though, revolve to the left and not to the right, like the Lightning Whelk (*above*). In this case the oddity will be the right-handed Lightning Whelk. Collectors are always searching for shells that spiral the opposite way to the rest of the species because they have a high commercial value.

When the garden spider makes its orb web in the

early morning on a bush, one of the first things it makes is a right-handed spiral from the centre of a silk rectangle woven with silk from the spinnerets. This is used as a base (like scaffolding on a building) and is destroyed by the spider when the web is eventually finished.

At first glance, the twining tendrils of garden pea plants seem tangled and disorganised. In fact, the tendrils spiral mathematically as they search for something to cling to for support. The springiness in the spiral gives the tendril surprising strength and flexibility. It takes a strong tug to dislodge the tendrils from a pea stick.

Man has copied this. The springs in our chairs and bed mattresses are just like the pea tendrils. Many other plants use the spiral, particularly climbing plants living in hedges, such as the woodbine, honeysuckle and bryony. The cauliflower heart and the pine cone display lovely spirals.

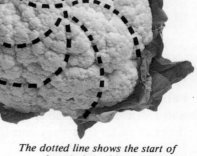

The dotted line shows the start of the spirals in this cauliflower

An Egyptian cobra

Curious uses of the spiral One of the oddest ways nature uses the spiral is displayed by snakes. Cobras and rattlesnakes form a spiral shape when threatened so that they can throw their body forward when striking.

Other examples of the spiral curve made by animals include the coil of an elephant's trunk (1), a chameleon's tail (2), the horns of an Argali Sheep (3), and the path taken by moths as they fly towards a candle flame (4). Moths do not look straight ahead because of their compound eyes. They make for the candle flame at a certain angle. They keep adjusting their path and fly in a spiral movement.

LEONARDO FIBONACCI OF PISA

Leonardo Fibonacci was a rich Italian merchant who lived in the city of Pisa in the thirteenth century. Leonardo was fascinated by mathematical problems and, as he travelled the world buying and selling goods, he studied mathematics in his spare time. Eventually he found time to write several learned books about his mathematical observations, and some of them were so good they were used in universities by students studying mathematics. In one book, *Liber Abaci,* which means The Book of Counting, Fibonacci described a series of numbers in a sequence which he discovered had numerous curious and interesting properties when applied to nature. It is for this discovery that Fibonacci is remembered, and the sequence of numbers is now known as the FIBONACCI SEQUENCE.

The Fibonacci Sequence
0 1 1 2 3 5 8 13 21 34 55 and so on.

Each number of this sequence, after the first two, is the sum of the preceding two numbers. That is to say:

$0 + 1 = 1$ $1 + 1 = 2$ $1 + 2 = 3$ $2 + 3 = 5$ $3 + 5 = 8$
$5 + 8 = 13$

The Fibonacci Sequence does not prove anything in Mathematics but is a number pattern that occurs frequently and unexpectedly in nature. For example, each type of flower growing wild in the countryside or cultivated in the garden has a characteristic number of petals.

The Fibonacci Sequence of numbers occurs
frequently in petal counts:

*2 petalled flowers are unusual,
but the Enchanter's Nightshade
that flowers in July in shaded
places has two petals (left).*

*3 petals occur in the lily family
and water-loving plants, such as
water soldier and arrow head
(below).*

*5 petals are the most common.
Examples include the buttercup
(left), woodsorrel and violets.*

*8 petals grow on the lesser
celandine (below).*

*13 petals are common and include
the ragwort (left) and mayweed
that grow on building clearance
areas.*

Asters have *21* petals. Flowers having *34* petals
include the field daisy and plantain that grow in
grassy areas.

Figwort also spirals

The Fibonacci Sequence is also apparent in the way leaves grow on plant stalks and the arrangement of young buds on a branch.

For example, look at the bottom bud on the branch of a pussy willow. If we call that bud 0, and then count up until we come to the bud directly over the first one, the number we get is usually from the Fibonacci Sequence. Also, as we work our way up the branch, count the number of times we revolve round it. This number, too, is usually a number from the sequence.

The buds grow on branches in a spiral pattern. The spiral can be seen by looking down on the branch from the top and turning the branch clockwise. Spirals like these are also noticeable in pine cones, pineapples, cauliflowers, and on some flowers like daisies and marigolds. The most well-known example of the spiral pattern in flowers develops in the giant sunflower *(right)* that towers over other flowers in our gardens.

After flowering, the yellow petals drop off, leaving behind a mass of sunflower seeds, which are set in a mathematical pattern. The seeds are in spiral formation, radiating from the centre to the outside of the sunflower head, both clockwise and

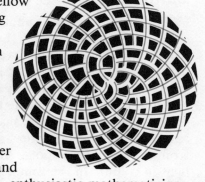

anti-clockwise. Patient, enthusiastic mathematicians have worked out that the total number of seeds is a number from the Fibonacci Sequence.

The sunflower seed is just the same kind of spiral mentioned earlier that occurs in snail shells and spider webs. This type of spiral does not alter in shape as it gets bigger and bigger, which perhaps explains why it is so often found in nature. As the creature inside the exquisite deep-sea chambered nautilus shell grows in size, the shell grows in spiral formation, and always remains an identically-proportioned home (right). The nautilus snail lives in the last chamber, which is the biggest. The empty chambers are used for buoyancy: the air in them keeps the creature upright under water.

MATHEMATICS IN TREE GROWTH

The trunk of a tree is another example of the circle occurring in nature. The tree trunk grows from a special layer in between the wood and the bark. This growing layer is called the *cambium layer,* made up of thousands of tiny cells that split and multiply throughout the tree's life. During each spring, the cambium layer makes new wood cells and bark cells, using water and minerals drawn up from the soil by the roots. All the new cells are light in colour. In the summer, when the tree grows more slowly because there is less water available, the cells are smaller, thicker and look dark. This is

Dry spell

Tree rings

Damp spell

Scar caused by fire

what creates the rings or circles that are seen when a tree is cut down. Each pairing of light and dark colours makes an *annual ring,* which means that we can estimate the age of the tree by counting. There is one ring for each year of the tree's life.

If the ring is wide, then the growth conditions during that year were good, with plenty of sunlight and moisture for the tree. If the ring is narrow, then the growth season was probably dry. By comparing rings from very old trees, scientists have compiled weather charts reaching back several hundreds of years. Normally, the annual rings could only be counted after a tree had been cut down. Now – fortunately for trees – small cores are taken out of the trunks with a boring tool. This does not damage the tree. The core shows all the annual rings.

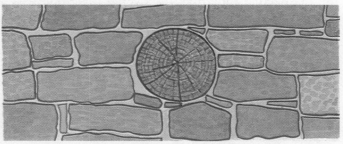

Archaeologists studying the Pueblo Indian cliff dwellings in the Western States of the USA wondered why and when the Pueblos suddenly deserted their ancestral homes. They found the answers to these questions through tree rings. By examining the tree poles (shown above) used by the

Pueblos for constructing their mud brick homes, the archaeologists deduced that a long and terrible drought forced the Indians to leave their miniature cities about 1290. The rings of the trees were in perfect condition, being beautifully and exactly preserved by the dry arid climate of the desert region, and they revealed that the trees had been cut before that date.

Tree rings can be read in other ways too, and give foresters a great deal of information about woodland history. Wet periods, dry spells, forest fires, prevailing winds, dense tree growth, and other items of information can be gleaned by looking at the pattern of tree ring development.

The Bristlecone Pine

In 1953, scientists in America who were studying the Bristlecone Pine tree, discovered that some growing in the mountains were 4000 years old, and realised that the gnarled, twisted Bristlecone Pine was the world's oldest living thing. One tree, dated by taking a core sample from its trunk, was as old as 4,600 years. That means its seed germinated about two and a half thousand years before Jesus Christ was born. The discovery astounded the scientists because the pine is so small, and only grows in the mountains at altitudes between 2400m and 3300m, where the soil is very poor and the weather often quite dreadful.

Carefully-prepared tree ring sections of the Pine are now used by archaeologists all over the USA when they uncover evidence of early civilisations. If

they find tree poles in a reasonable condition, they can compare the tree ring patterns with the Bristlecone Pine, and find out approximately when the dwelling was inhabited.

The giant Sierra Redwood is the biggest tree in the world and was once thought to be the oldest. One redwood that grows in Humboldt State Park in California is 111m tall and over 2000 years old. Another, known affectionately as the General Sherman, is 83m tall, 35m wide round the base of the trunk, and is over 3000 years old.

Oak
30 metres

Redwood
111 metres

Bristlecone
Pine
12 metres

DATING HEDGEROWS

Hedgerows are a well-established feature of the countryside. Some have been made from stone while others were planted. Whatever their foundation, they are a haven for plants and small animals, giving robins and wrens, voles and shrews, food and shelter. Many of the old hedges were planted over five hundred years ago and have changed very little since.

A scientist called Dr Max Hooper has studied hedges and the plants and animals that live in them. He discovered a very interesting mathematical aspect in the way hedges develop. He found that, in

Hawthorn   *Honeysuckle*   *Dogrose*   *Eld*

general, a hedge about a hundred years old has only one or two types of shrubs growing in it. A hedge two hundred years old has two or three shrub types. A hedge one thousand years old has about ten different kinds of shrubs. From this information Dr Hooper has worked out a simple mathematical formula for finding out the age of hedges in our countryside. Just measure thirty metres of hedgerow, count the number of shrub species growing, multiply by a hundred and you have the approximate age of the hedge. The date can often be verified by checking local records.

Ash

CRYSTALS

So far we have looked at the geometric mathematics in the forms of *animate* (which means 'living') things. Geometric precision helps survival. Geometry is also common in the *inanimate* world.

Spectacular minerals and crystals that lie underground in mines and caves have fascinated man throughout the ages. They are often brilliantly coloured and sparkle in the light as much as the

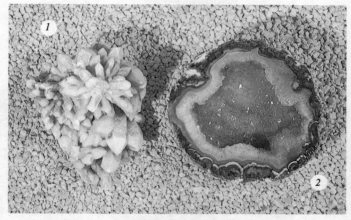

1 Milky quartz cluster (North Wales)   2 Amethyst geode (Arizona)

precious gemstones that are cut from them. Crystals form yet another intriguing and exquisite example of nature's mathematics.

In the eighteenth century, rock crystals were called 'The Flowers of the Kingdom' by an enthusiastic collector called Abbé René Haüy of France who spent all his life studying the remarkable crystal shapes he dug from the earth.

1 Smoky quartz geode   2 Milky quartz geode

3 and 4 Two varieties of calcite

Before and since Haüy's time, crystals have been mined, hoarded, sold, bartered and exchanged, and brought out the greed in men. Diamonds are among

1 Quartz

2 Double ended "Herkimer" Rock diamond (from Herkimer County, New York)

the rarest crystals and perfect specimens fetch huge prices in the jewel market. The word *'crystal'* comes from the Greek word 'krystallos' which in turn is derived from 'kryos', which means icy cold. The early Greeks believed that transparent quartz crystals were made from ice frozen so hard it would never thaw out.

Crystals are *polygons,* which means many-sided, and come in a variety of mathematical shapes. Many are so perfect and geometric in appearance they seem to have been cut by a master craftsman. In 1669, Nicolaus Steno's fascination for their individuality led him to notice that for any crystal of a given mineral, the angles measured between the crystal faces were always exactly the same. This means that any crystal of quartz, for instance, when measured with a simple instrument (below) called a *goniometer,* (gonio means angle and meter means measure) has the same set of angles. This is important to geologists because not all

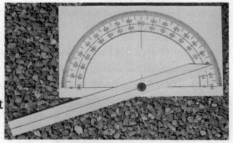

crystals grow perfectly and it helps them to identify specimens found by others on field trips. Different varieties of minerals have different crystal shapes and the crystals are classified by the number of faces they possess. Geologists have worked out six crystal systems: Isometric; Tetragonal; Orthorhombic; Monoclinic; Triclinic; and Hexagonal.

The best crystals are formed in rock cavities. They are always being formed in nature. Our planet Earth is surrounded by gases and is always losing water from its surface. The movement of water on and in its crust mixes minerals, and the fierce heat in the earth's centre is periodically forcing molten rock towards the surface. The minerals in the hot water are left in crystal form when the water evaporates. Large crystals are formed when the evaporation is slow and gradual. Some crystals can be grown in the laboratory. These are called synthetic crystals and are used in industry. Quartz crystals are grown on a large scale because they have many uses. Small crystals of salt and sugar can be grown in the kitchen as follows.

Carefully place one tablespoonful of salt or sugar in a clean jam jar and add two tablespoonfuls of hot, boiled water. Stir the mixture until all the salt or sugar has dissolved. Then pour the solution on to a white saucer and watch carefully. After a short time little crystals appear on the saucer.

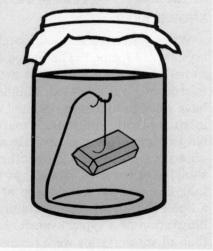

The crystal in the illustration is more complicated and is usually grown by chemistry students.

Growing a crystal by evaporation

43

SNOWFLAKES

When water freezes, exquisitely-shaped ice crystals are formed. The incredible forms of snowflakes were first seen in detail when the microscope was invented. Hundreds of pictures have since been drawn, painted and photographed, in attempts to capture their mathematical precision. No two snowflakes are exactly alike. The first observer who tried to show others just what snowflakes (or snowcrystals, as scientists call them) look like was the Archbishop of Uppsala. He wrote a book in Italy in 1555 containing a woodcut illustration of a typical snowcrystal. He discovered that all snowcrystals were hexagons (six-sided) and yet all were different from each other in design.

For over fifty years in the early part of the 20th century, Wilson Bentley caught and photographed thousands of snowflakes, and then gave all his pictures to scientists to study. His work with snowflakes earned him his nickname of Snowflake Bentley.

LEARNING FROM NATURE

Through scientists' observations and study, we know that the geometric mathematics in nature is concerned with giving living things shapes that are practical, to help species to survive. The bee, for

example, is a perfect flying machine. The wings are exactly the right measurement required to produce the energy to lift the insect off the ground, and the right shape for flying, once airborne.

The jay's beak is the ideal size, shape and strength for cracking the hard shells of hazel nuts. Nature's failures die if their form is not practical and does not help them to fit in with their

environment. Some change their life style. The ostrich has reached such a size that it is impossible for it to fly. Yet nature has compensated by giving the bird great speed of foot to escape predators. We know that the geometric forms we see today are the result of changes made over millions of years.

Man is an intelligent being. He can reason. He has used nature's creations as models. His designs change and develop from simple beginnings, just like nature. As tastes change and new materials are invented, new designs are created.

Since the first trial and error discovery of the best shape for a tool from a piece of bone or stone, the shapes of many man-made things are mathematically worked out before they are produced. They are logical shapes.

Nature's exquisite and intricate forms have taught us a great deal about the combination of beauty, function and strength. In the home, our kitchen pots and pans, tools and gadgets, deliberately follow the basic geometric patterns, combining beauty and strength.

47

Man, like nature, attempts to make the most of materials at hand and knows the limit of their usefulness. As buildings are mathematical structures, architects and builders work out which shape and size would use the available building material wisely. Modern tower blocks, lamp-posts and car parks are pleasing to look at, are strong, and carry out their required purpose. They are also built with the minimum amount of concrete. The spacing of the bases of structures is important. The long thin legs of a spider are spaced so that they can support the spider's body. Pylons that carry

electric cables are similar. They are said to be built from steel and air. That is, the fine steel rods are placed in such a way that the structure has maximum strength for the material used.

Boat builders learned a great deal from the streamlining of fish. A yacht's sails are like a large albatross' wing; birds' wings and tails have helped man to build and fly aircraft. A bird's wing is a marvellous feat of engineering. The feather is light, yet strong enough to lift a bird and to resist the buffeting from the wind. A microscopic view of the wing bones would show that the bones are hollow and lighter than the weight of the feathers. This formation has given inspiration to our bridge builders. The design of our metal bridges looks very

Section of bird's bone

Ironbridge

similar to the inside of a wing bone. The first bridge made from iron was built across the River Severn in 1779. Understanding the strains and stresses of a bird's wing helped the engineer with the problems of using iron for the bridge. The design of the bridge has a criss-cross pattern, like the internal pattern of a bird's bone.

49

A cross-section of a human bone (*above*) shows that it is hollow, with supports stretching from one side to the other. The supports give the bone strength. In 1866 an engineer called Culmann saw a surgeon friend slice a section of human bone. He noticed how nature strengthened the bone and he used the same design for a huge crane.

The largest modern cranes still use nature's principle

Complete skeletons of large creatures like horses have shown engineers how to get over major building problems. The structure of the gigantic

Forth Bridge

Forth Bridge, opened in 1890, resembles the internal design of a skeleton.

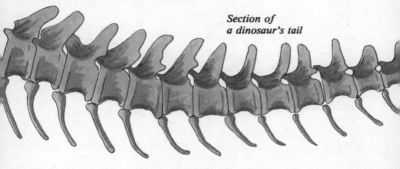

Section of a dinosaur's tail

We learn from nature. Not many of nature's creations are failures. It is true that some plants and an occasional animal are becoming extinct. This is due to pollution and over-killing, and not to a fault of their shape or size.

Mathematics has helped nature to create success in its living things. Mathematics helps man to create machines to improve his life. Nature is a master builder. Can this be said of man?

INDEX